I Know How!

Learning to Follow Directions

Arnold Cheyney
University of Miami
Coral Gables, Florida

Jeanne Cheyney

Scott, Foresman and Company
Glenview, Illinois   London

 **Good Year Books** are available for preschool through grade 12 and for every basic curriculum subject plus many enrichment areas. For more Good Year Books, contact your local bookseller or educational dealer. For a complete catalog with information about other Good Year Books, please write:

Good Year Books
Department GYB
1900 East Lake Avenue
Glenview, Illinois 60025

ISBN 0-673-18751-9

Copyright © 1987 Scott, Foresman and Company.
All Rights Reserved.
Printed in the United States of America.

2 3 4 5 6—MAL—92 91 90 89 88 87

No part of the book may be reproduced in any form or by any means, except those portions intended for classroom use, without permission in writing from the publisher.

Contents

Introduction v

HOME

Brushing Your Teeth 1
Changing a Light Bulb 2
Decorating the Christmas Tree 3
Doing Homework 4
Eating Cereal for Breakfast 5
Frying an Egg for Breakfast 6
Making a Peanut Butter and Jelly Sandwich 7
Making Brown Sugar Toast 8
Making Your Bed 9
Putting on Your Clothes 10
Scrubbing the Floor 11
Setting the Table for Dinner 12
Sewing on a Button 13
Shopping at the Supermarket 14
Washing Dishes 15
Washing the Car 16
Washing the Laundry 17
Washing Your Face 18
Washing Your Hair 19

SCHOOL

Adding Boys and Girls 20
Alphabetizing Words 21
Checking out a Library Book 22
Cleaning out a School Desk 23
Doing a Science Experiment 24
Eating in the Cafeteria 25
Finding a Word in the Dictionary 26
Finding the Continents on the Globe 27
Going to School 28
Passing Back Papers for the Teacher 29
Playing at Recess 30
Pledging Allegiance to Flag and Country 31
Riding the School Bus 32
Sharpening Pencils 33
Subtracting Apples 34
Taking a Note to the Office 35
Using the Overhead Projector 36
Washing the Chalkboard 37
Writing a Letter 38

AROUND AND ABOUT

Building a Campfire 39
Building a Snowman 40
Crossing at the Traffic Light 41
Curling Your Hair 42
Drawing a Comic Face 43
Exercising the Aerobic Way 44
Feeding a Pet 45
Going Roller Skating 46
Introducing a Friend 47
Making a Paper Bag Puppet 48
Making Angels in the Snow 49
Making Clay Shapes 50
Making Paper Doll Dresses 51
Making Popcorn 52
Ordering a Meal at a Restaurant 53
Planting Seeds 54
Roasting Marshmallows 55
Shooting a Basket 56
Tying Your Shoes 57

Introduction

Every teacher, at one time or another, has said to her students: "If you would only follow my directions!"

Even adults, however, have trouble when they try to follow directions for assembling a new bicycle or preparing a no-fail cake recipe. Despite the fact that following directions is a skill that everyone is supposed to master, few of us get the concentrated meaningful experiences we need in order to do so.

The activity pages in *I Know How!* focus on real-life rather than abstract situations. These pages require students to give logical, sequential explanations of everyday events in a systematic way.

The basic format for using these activities to implement a language arts approach to following directions involves four steps:

1. Students *read* the directions on an activity page.
2. Students *discuss* various ways to follow the directions.
3. Students *listen* in order to determine the approach they will use.
4. Students *write* the directions in their own words.

Because writing impresses information more solidly on the mind than either reading or hearing, *I Know How!* emphasizes student writing of directions.

Teaching Tips and Techniques

1. Use the activities with individuals or small groups.
2. Before passing out an activity page (or pages), ask the students to give directions orally for the assigned activity(ies)—e.g., making your bed, washing dishes, sharpening pencils.
3. Point out that activity page illustrations provide ideas and clues for answering the questions at the bottom of the page.
4. Divide the students into small groups to discuss possible ways to write the directions for a given activity.
5. Tape record answers to activity page questions and then play the answers back to the class for comments.
6. Discuss the range of correct answers possible on many of the activity pages.
7. Allow for answers that range from single words to phrases to sentences or even narrative. The fullness of student answers will depend on individual language maturity.
8. Encourage students to put their own names in the activity page stories in place of the ones already there; doing so helps many students write from their own point of view.

9. Encourage students to change the activity pages in order to reflect their own experiences. For example, a student may want to add (or substitute) directions for preparing bacon, grits, or toast when working on "Frying an Egg for Breakfast."
10. After the children complete the directions, use an appropriate activity page as a story starter. Students can finish the story on the back of the sheet.
11. Emphasize that students should revise their answers until both they and the teacher are satisfied that they have done their best work.
12. Use the dialogue found on some activity pages as models for learning where to place punctuation marks.
13. As a class project, try to list as many instances as possible in which people are expected to follow directions during the course of an ordinary day. Use the list for class discussion as well as for reading and writing assignments.
14. Have the students illustrate some of the situations on the list. After discussing the situations and illustrations, students can create their own written explanations.
15. Encourage students familiar with the **I Know How!** concept to take activity pages home with them to discuss and complete with parents; pages from the HOME section would be particularly appropriate.
16. To help children connect ideas when writing directions, copy the following chart of linking words and numbers onto the chalkboard. If students think of other connecting words, add them to the chart.

	Numbers		*Linking Words*	
1.	1st	first	afterwards	later
2.	2nd	second	immediately	last
3.	3rd	third	finally	until
4.	4th	fourth	now	and
5.	5th	fifth	next	meanwhile
6.	6th	sixth	soon	in addition to

Eating Cereal for Breakfast

Wanda liked eating cereal for breakfast every day. She could almost prepare it with her eyes closed.

This is what Wanda did every morning.

On the lines below, write what Wanda had to do before she could eat her cereal.

_____

_____

_____

_____

Frying an Egg for Breakfast

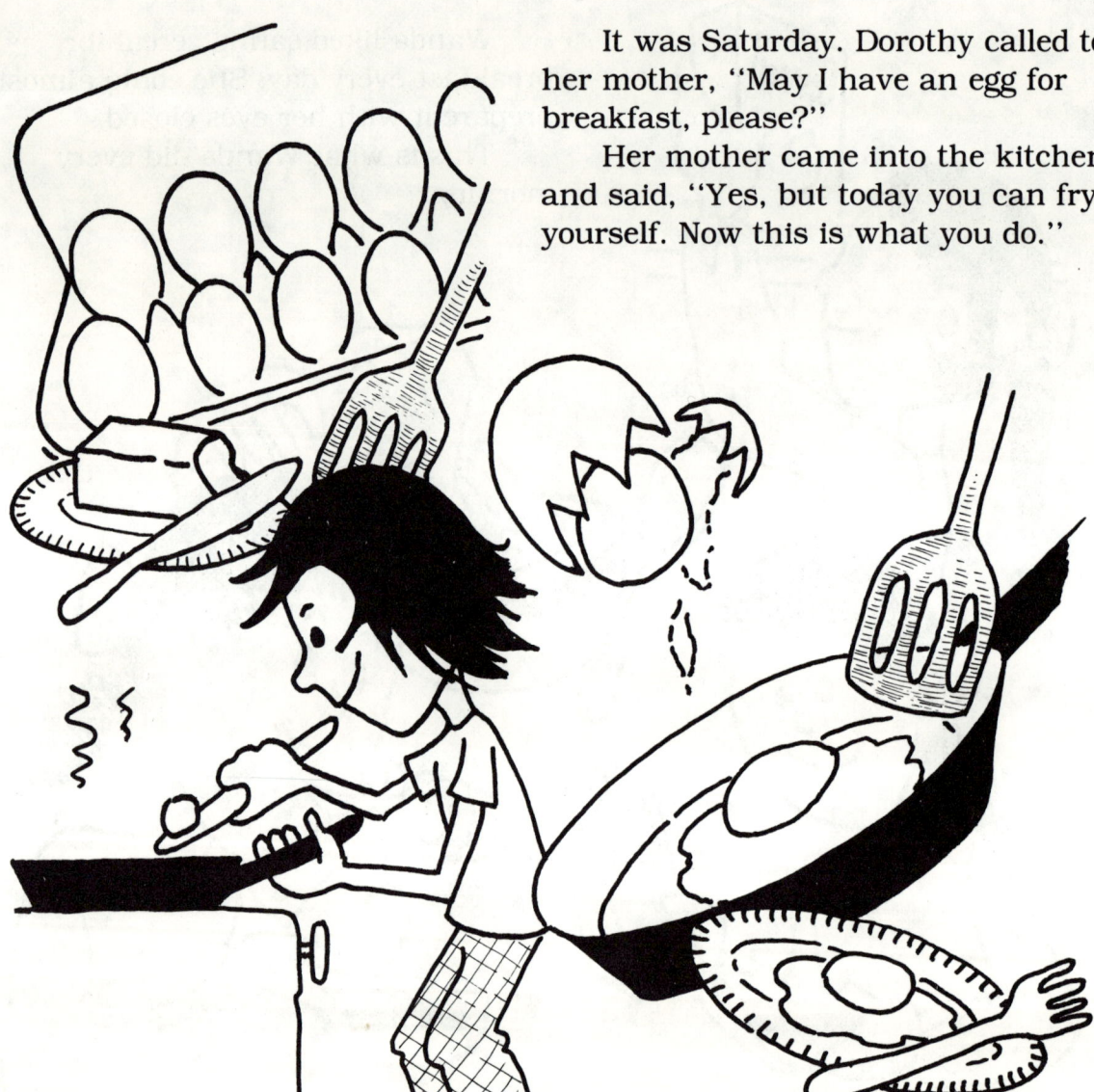

It was Saturday. Dorothy called to her mother, "May I have an egg for breakfast, please?"

Her mother came into the kitchen and said, "Yes, but today you can fry it yourself. Now this is what you do."

What did Dorothy's mother say about frying an egg?

_____

_____

_____

_____

_____

Making a Peanut Butter and Jelly Sandwich

Jean was hungry, really starved. She asked, "Mother, may I make a peanut butter and jelly sandwich?"

"Yes," her mother replied, "but clean up when you're finished."

Jean smacked her lips. She could taste the sandwich already.

What did Jean have to do to prepare her sandwich?

_____

_____

_____

_____

8 • HOME   Name _____

Making Brown Sugar Toast

Alice loved warm buttered toast with brown sugar on it. Sometimes she would sprinkle a little cinnamon on top, too. Alice liked to drink a cup of hot chocolate when she ate her toast.

What did Alice have to do to make brown sugar toast?

_____

_____

_____

_____

_____

Making Your Bed

Don looked at his bed. It was a mess.
"I think I'll surprise Mom and make the bed myself," he said aloud. Then he thought to himself, What do I do first?

How did Don make his bed?

_____

_____

_____

_____

Putting on Your Clothes

Philip slept late one morning.

"Philip," his mother called, "you'll have to hurry or you'll be late for school!"

"I'll be right there," he said. "I have my clothes all ready to put on."

On the lines below, write how Philip dressed himself that morning.

_____

_____

_____

_____

_____

Scrubbing the Floor

Gail spilled orange juice on the kitchen floor.

"Oh, Mom, what can I do?" she asked. "It was an accident."

Her mother smiled. "I know it was," she said, "but you'll have to clean it up. You've watched me scrub the floors. What do I do?"

Gail got busy right away.

What did Gail do to clean the orange juice off the floor?

_____

_____

_____

_____

Setting the Table for Dinner

It was Judy's job each night to set the table. As soon as she came home from school, she got busy. Within minutes she had the table set for her parents, her two sisters, and herself.

What did Judy have to do to set the table for dinner?

_____

_____

_____

_____

Sewing on a Button

Tim was getting ready to go to school. As he put on his shirt, he noticed that a button was missing. He called to his mother for help, but she had gone to the store.

What will I do? he thought. He tried to remember how his mother sewed on buttons.

Finally he said, "I can do it myself."

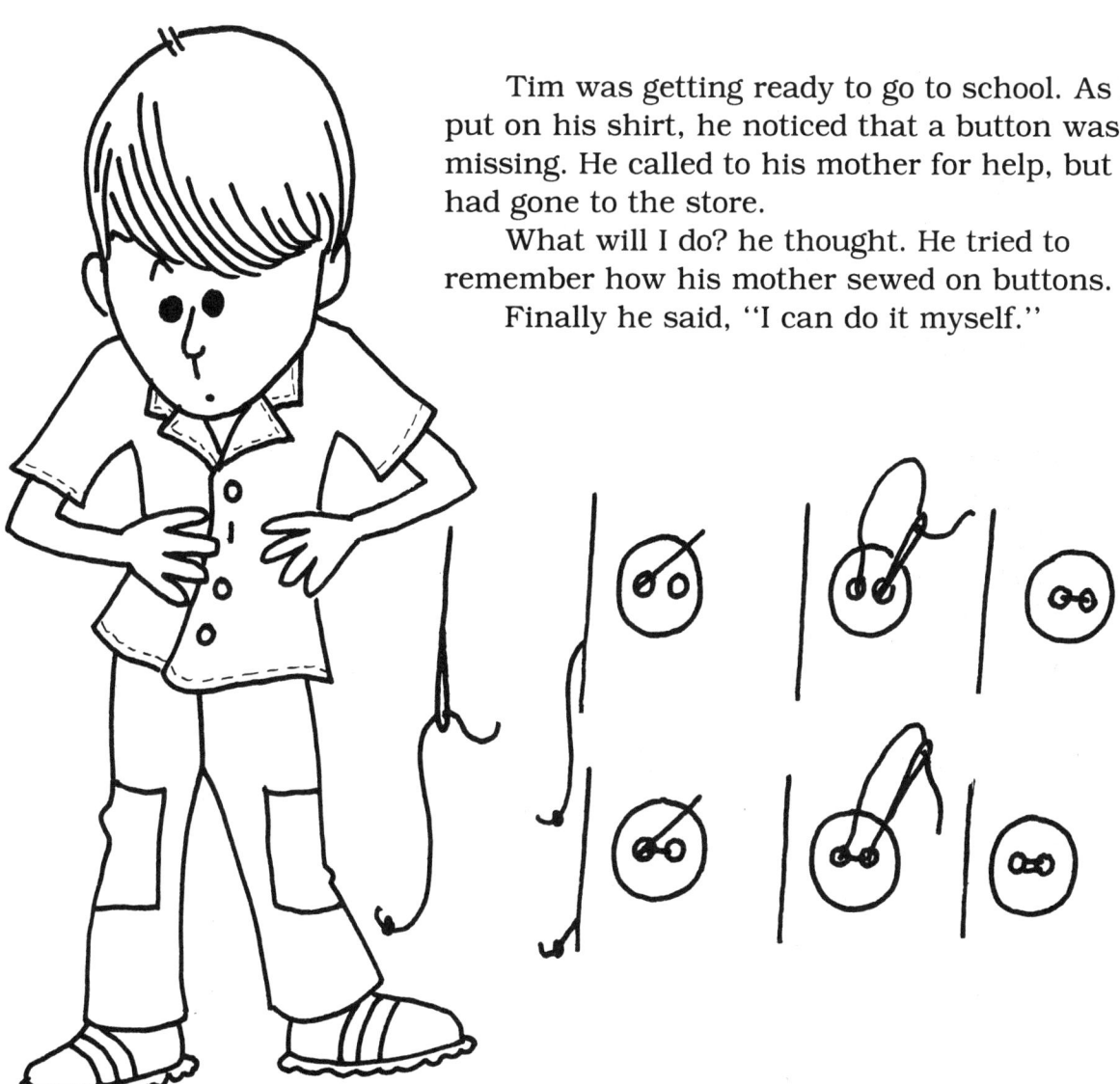

On the lines below, write the steps—in the correct order—that Tim followed to sew on his button.

_____

_____

_____

_____

14 • HOME   Name _____

Shopping at the Supermarket

"Robert, come here please," called his mother. "We're out of milk and groceries. I've made a list of what we need. Here's the list and a ten dollar bill. Now, be careful, and hurry right back," she said.

Robert went straight to the supermarket. This is what he did when he got there.

Write what Robert did when he went to the supermarket. Be sure to put everything in the right order.

_____
_____
_____
_____
_____

Name _____   HOME • 15

Washing Dishes

"Since today is your birthday, Mom, I'll do the dinner dishes," said Jack.

"Why, thank you, Jack," she replied.

Jack went to the kitchen to get everything ready.

Write what Jack did to wash the dinner dishes.

_____

_____

_____

_____

Washing the Car

"Bill," his father said, "the car really needs a good washing. Would you take care of it for me this morning?"

This was Bill's big chance. He had never washed the car by himself before.

"I sure will, Dad." Bill jumped up and got started right away.

What did Bill have to do to wash the car?

_____

_____

_____

_____

Washing the Laundry

Daisy's mother was not feeling well.

"I'll do the laundry today, Mom," Daisy said. "I've watched you, so I know exactly what to do."

"I appreciate your wanting to help, Daisy," her mother replied. "But before you begin, tell me step by step what you are going to do."

On the lines below, write what Daisy told her mother.

_____

_____

_____

_____

Washing Your Face

After he played all day, Jason had a dirty face.

His father said, "Wash your face!"

His mother said, "Wash your face!"

My face must really be dirty, Jason thought.

His older sister shouted, "Don't forget to wash your neck and scrub behind your ears!"

Write what Jason had to do to get his face, ears, and neck clean.

_____

_____

_____

_____

_____

Washing Your Hair

Mary enjoyed washing her hair. One night, when no one else wanted the shower, she got out her shampoo. Tonight Mary would really get her hair clean.

Write the steps—in order—that Mary followed when she washed her hair.

_____

_____

_____

_____

_____

Adding Boys and Girls

"Is everyone here?" Jenny asked, looking around the classroom. "I'd better count. First, I'll count the boys, then the girls," she said.

Girls ___
Boys ___
In all ___

Write what Jenny did to find out how many children were in her classroom that day.

_____
_____
_____
_____

Name _____ SCHOOL • 21

Alphabetizing Words

The teacher gave Connie, Carl, and Esther three words apiece to put in alphabetical order on the chalkboard.

What did each one do to alphabetize his or her list?

cat
cry
cup

came
cart
castle

came
camel
camera

Write what Connie, Carl, and Esther did to alphabetize their three words.

_____
_____
_____
_____

Checking out a Library Book

While watching TV, Peter heard about a book that interested him. He asked his teacher about the book.

"I think that book is in the library," Peter's teacher told him. "You may go and get it now, if you wish."

What did Peter do to get the book from the library?

_____

_____

_____

_____

Cleaning out a School Desk

Gloria's desk was a mess.

"You must clean out your desk and have your things back in neatly before lunch," her teacher said.

Gloria got busy right away. Soon she had filled the trash can with things from her desk. She finished just before the lunch bell rang.

How did Gloria get her desk in order so quickly?

On the lines below, write what Gloria did to clean out her desk.

_____

_____

_____

_____

Doing a Science Experiment

Of all her subjects, June liked science the best. But today she was having trouble figuring out what had happened in her candle experiment.

Her teacher smiled and said, "You did everything right, June. What's the matter?"

"The candle went out," June answered.

"Of course it did. It was supposed to go out," her teacher said. "You did the experiment correctly."

Write the steps June followed to do her experiment. Then explain why the candle went out.

_____

_____

_____

_____

Eating in the Cafeteria

Mark and Sarah liked eating lunch in the school cafeteria. Whenever a new student entered their classroom, they showed him or her how to get lunch.

On the lines below, explain how a new student would get lunch in your school cafeteria.

_____

_____

_____

_____

_____

Finding a Word in the Dictionary

Jill could not spell a word that she needed for her story. The word she needed was "separate."

What will I do? she thought. Then she knew. Jill went to the bookcase and got out the dictionary.

This is how she found the correct way to spell the word she needed.

Imagine that you have a friend who needs to find the word "separate" in the dictionary. On the lines below, tell your friend what to do.

_____

_____

_____

_____

Finding the Continents on the Globe

Walter wanted to know the names of all the Earth's continents. He looked up the word "continent" in the dictionary. There he found a list of the continents.

After writing down the names of all the continents, Walter put away the dictionary. Then he went over to the globe and found where each continent is located.

List the names of the continents on the lines below. Then explain how you would find them on a globe.

_____
_____
_____
_____

28 • SCHOOL   Name _____

Going to School

Jim lived a few blocks from school. His cousin asked him, "Jim, how do you get to your school?"

Jim thought and thought. How do I get to my school? he asked himself.

Can you tell someone who has never been to your school how to get there from your home?

On the lines below, explain how to get to your school from where you live.

_____

_____

_____

_____

From *I Know How! Learning to Follow Directions.* Copyright © 1987 Scott, Foresman and Company.

Passing Back Papers for the Teacher

"Tom," Mr. Johnson called, "it's your turn to pass back papers to the class."

"Yes, sir, Mr. Johnson," Tom said politely.

Tom knew the best and quickest way to pass back papers for the teacher.

Describe how Tom passed back papers to the class.

_____

_____

_____

_____

Playing at Recess

The children in Mrs. Turner's class enjoyed recess. They jumped rope, played ball, or climbed the jungle gym.

Of these three, what is your favorite recess activity?

After you choose your favorite recess activity, write the directions for playing it on the lines below.

_____

_____

_____

_____

_____

Pledging Allegiance to Flag and Country

The first things that Lisa's class did each day were to say the Pledge of Allegiance and sing the "Star Spangled Banner."

Lisa knew what to do each morning without anyone telling her.

Tell what Lisa did when it was time to say the Pledge of Allegiance and sing the "Star Spangled Banner."

_____

_____

_____

_____

Riding the School Bus

The children waited at the school bus stop. Finally, the bus came.

The bus driver opened the door and smiled. "Careful! Watch your step," he called out.

The bus did not start up until all the children were aboard and in their seats.

What rules do boys and girls have to follow if they want to ride the school bus? Write the rules—in the correct order—on the lines below.

_____

_____

_____

_____

Sharpening Pencils

"Teacher," said George, "my pencils need sharpening."

"You may go to the pencil sharpener and sharpen them," she said.

George picked up three pencils and headed for the pencil sharpener.

What did George do next?

Write what George did to sharpen his pencils.

_____

_____

_____

_____

Subtracting Apples

"Lois, would you please go to the chalkboard and do the subtraction problem I put there?" Mrs. Smith asked.

Oh, I hope I get it right, Lois thought.

When Lois finished the problem, Mrs. Smith said, "Fine. Now explain to the class how you did the subtraction problem."

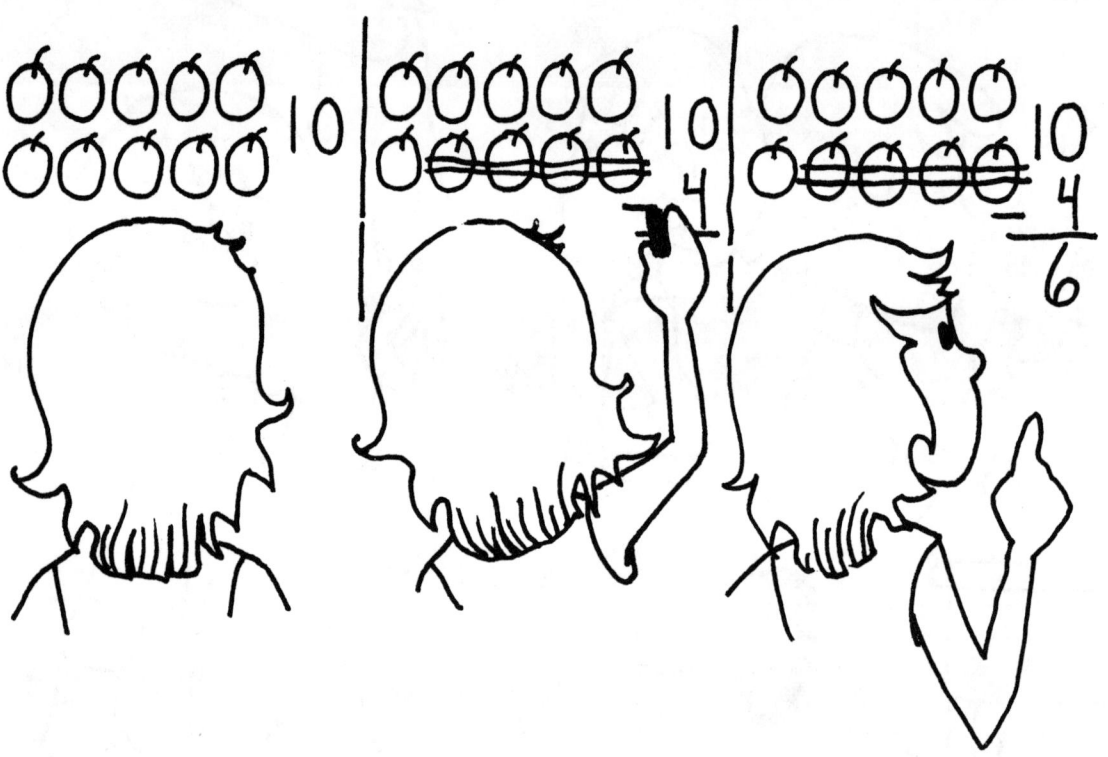

On the lines below, tell how Lois explained the subtraction problem to the class.

_____

_____

_____

_____

Taking a Note to the Office

Melinda's teacher asked her to take a note to the school office.

"Come right back," said the teacher.

Melinda said she would.

How did Melinda get to the office and back?

On the lines below, describe how Melinda would go from the classroom to the office in *your* school. Be sure to include the people she would meet along the way.

_____

_____

_____

_____

36 • SCHOOL

Using the Overhead Projector

"Henry," said Henry's teacher Mrs. Adams, "I want you to teach the class how to use the overhead projector. Here is a felt pen and some acetates for making transparencies. The overhead projector is in the closet."

How did Henry teach the class to use the overhead projector?

_____

_____

_____

_____

Washing the Chalkboard

Karen asked her teacher for permission to wash the chalkboard because it was so dusty.

"Yes, you may," her teacher replied.

Karen gathered everything she needed and started at once. Soon the chalkboard was sparkling clean.

What did Karen do to get the board so clean?

On the lines below, write what Karen did to wash the chalkboard.

_____

_____

_____

_____

Writing a Letter

Steve had not seen Jerry for a long time.
  I should write him a letter, Steve thought.
  This is what Steve wrote.

> 1234 Peach Street
> Anywhere, OH 44614
> November 30, 19—

Dear Jerry,
  I miss you. I hope we can get together before next year.
  My parents bought me a dog. I call him "Holler" because he makes so much noise.
  Please write back to me.

> Your friend,
>
> Steve

  On the back of this sheet, give the directions for writing a letter to a friend. Then write a real letter to one of your friends, following the model shown below.

(Your address) _____
(Date) _____

(Greeting) _____,
(Body) _____
_____
_____
_____
_____
_____

(Closing) _____,
(Your name) _____

Building a Campfire

John wanted to learn how to build a campfire.

"I'll teach you in the backyard," his dad said, "but you must obey the rules of safety."

Later, when John was camping in the woods, he remembered what his father had taught him about building a campfire.

What did John's father teach him about building a campfire?

_____

_____

_____

_____

Building a Snowman

David patted some snow into a ball. The snow was damp, good for building a snowman. David began rolling his snowball over the ground. Soon he had built a snowman.

On the lines below, describe how David built a snowman.

_____

_____

_____

_____

_____

Crossing at the Traffic Light

Denise walked down the street to school. When she reached the corner, the traffic light was red. She knew what to do to get across the street safely.

What did Denise do? Write the steps—in the correct order—that Denise followed to cross the street safely.

_____

_____

_____

_____

Curling Your Hair

One morning, Ann looked at herself in the mirror.

"I think I'll curl my hair today," she said aloud.

She got everything ready, and then this is what she did.

How did Ann curl her hair? On the lines below, tell what she did. Be sure to keep the steps in the right order.

_____

_____

_____

_____

_____

Name _____ AROUND AND ABOUT • 43

Drawing a Comic Face

Betty enjoyed drawing pictures. She copied the cartoons that she found in the newspaper, and then she made up her own cartoons.

She looked carefully at the different eyes, mouths, ears, and noses in the comics. She used these face parts when she drew her own cartoon figures.

When her friends wanted to draw cartoons, too, Betty showed them how. Pretend that you are one of Betty's friends. Make a comic face below.

Now imagine that a friend wants to know how you drew your comic face. Write the directions on the lines below.

_____

_____

_____

_____

Exercising the Aerobic Way

Elaine asked her mother if she could learn to do aerobics.

"Yes, you can," her mother said. "I have a video tape on aerobic exercising that you can use."

Elaine put the video tape in the VCR and then followed the directions she saw on her TV screen.

What did Elaine do to learn aerobic exercising?

_____

_____

_____

_____

Feeding a Pet

Vanessa loved her dog, Spot. She fed him every day.

One day, Spot was very hungry. He barked and barked for Vanessa to prepare his meal.

This is what Vanessa did.

On the lines below, tell what Vanessa did to feed Spot.

_____

_____

_____

_____

46 • AROUND AND ABOUT   Name _____

Going Roller Skating

Martha loved to roller skate. Every week she went to the roller skating rink.

Martha saved money from her allowance to pay for her time at the rink.

What does Martha have to do before she can begin skating?

_____
_____
_____
_____
_____

Introducing a Friend

The first time that Roger came over to Wayne's house to play, Wayne said, "Roger, I want you to meet my dad. He's the greatest!"

Just then, Wayne's father came into the front room. Wayne exclaimed, "Here he is now!"

What did Wayne say when he introduced his father to Roger?

Describe how Wayne introduced his father and Roger to each other.

_____

_____

_____

_____

Making a Paper Bag Puppet

Anita enjoyed making paper bag puppets. She even taught her little brother to make them. Then the two children put on shows for the neighborhood.

Tell how Anita made her paper bag puppets. Be sure to put all the steps in the right order.

_____

_____

_____

_____

Making Angels in the Snow

Beth could hardly wait for the first snow of the winter. She loved to make angels in the snow.

One day it began to snow. "Mother, Mother!" Beth called. "It's snowing. May I go outside?"

"Yes," her mother answered, "but first dress warmly."

What did Beth do first? Then how did she make angels in the snow?

_____

_____

_____

_____

Making Clay Shapes

Harold enjoyed playing with clay. He made all kinds of shapes. One day he decided that he would make the best clay figure he had ever made.

He took out the clay, held it in his hands, and thought for a moment. Then he began.

What did Harold decide to make? How did he make it?

_____
_____
_____
_____

Making Paper Doll Dresses

Vicki was always busy making dresses for her paper doll. She made party dresses and play clothes. Sometimes she made clothes that her doll could wear to church and school. Since the doll was made of cardboard, Vicki could stand it up on a table for everyone to see.

How did Vicki make the dresses for her paper doll?

_____

_____

_____

_____

Making Popcorn

Larry loved popcorn. In fact, he enjoyed making it almost as much as he loved eating it.

This is how Larry popped corn.

On the lines below, explain how Larry made popcorn. Be sure to put the steps in the right order.

_____

_____

_____

_____

_____

Ordering a Meal at a Restaurant

Nick and his father went to eat at a restaurant. They looked at the menu.

"What do you want, Nick?" his father asked.

Nick said, "I think I'll have a salad, a hamburger with everything on it, french fries, and iced tea."

When the waitress came to take the order, Nick's father told her what they wanted.

Write what you think Nick's father told the waitress.

_____

_____

_____

_____

Planting Seeds

It was springtime. Charles planted beans and other seeds. He enjoyed watching them grow.

"Tell me how you planted your beans," his dad said.

"Well, this is what I did," Charles answered.

List the steps—in the right order—that Charles followed when he planted his beans.

_____

_____

_____

_____

Roasting Marshmallows

Scott made a wood fire in his backyard. When the fire burned down, he decided to roast marshmallows. Soon Scott was ready to roast marshmallows over the fire.

What did Scott have to do before he could roast marshmallows?

_____
_____
_____
_____

Shooting a Basket

Michael enjoyed playing basketball. One of his friends called to him, "Michael, show me how to shoot the ball through the hoop."

Michael smiled and said, "Just watch!"

He dribbled down the court and made a perfect layup. His friend was amazed.

How did Michael do that?

On the lines below, write what Michael had to do to make the basket.

_____

_____

_____

_____

Tying Your Shoes

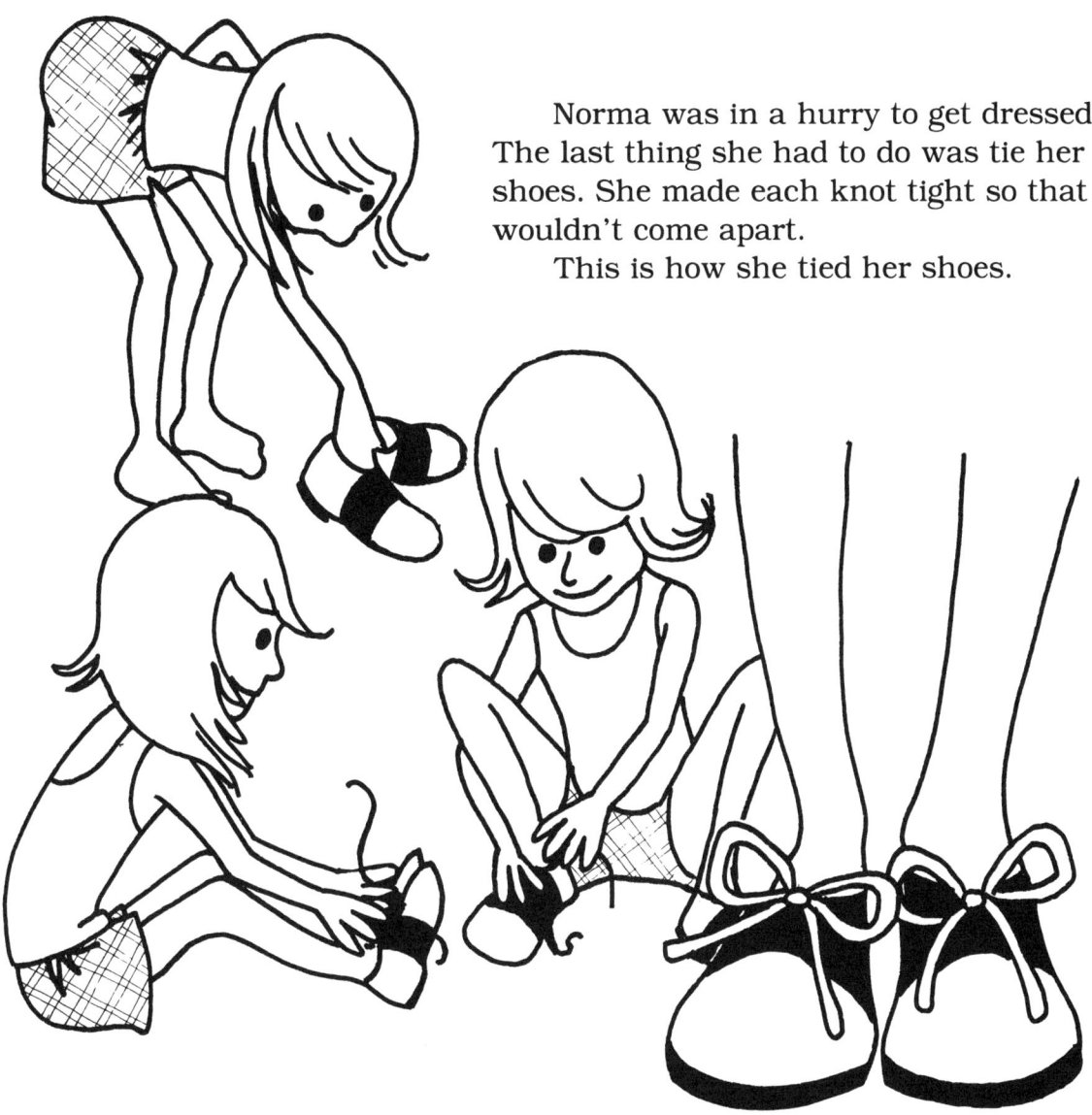

Norma was in a hurry to get dressed. The last thing she had to do was tie her shoes. She made each knot tight so that it wouldn't come apart.

This is how she tied her shoes.

List the steps—in the right order—that Norma followed when she tied her shoes.

_____

_____

_____

_____

_____